CW00344880

PRESENTED TO

Ashley

BY

Mark, Debbie, Robert, Val + Jim

ON THE OCCASION OF

Confirmation on 14-12-1999

A Little Prayer Diary

CHRISTOPHER HERBERT

HarperCollins*Publishers*

HarperCollins*Publishers*
77–85 Fulham Palace Road, London W6 8JB

Previously published as *Be Thou My Vision* in 1985
by Collins Liturgical Publications
This edition first published in Great Britain in 1996 by
HarperCollins*Publishers*

1 3 5 7 9 10 8 6 4 2

Copyright © 1985, 1996 by Christopher Herbert

A catalogue record for this book is
available from the British Library

The publishers are grateful to the
British and Foreign Bible Society for permission
to quote from the *Good News Bible*, published by
the Bible Societies/Collins, © American Bible Society 1976.
Various prayers from the *Alternative Prayer Book 1980* are
© the Central Board of Finance of the Church of England
and are reproduced with permission.

000 62780129

Printed and bound in Great Britain by
Woolnough Bookbinding Ltd, Irthlingborough, Northamptonshire

Contents

Introduction

Christian prayer is based on the knowledge that in Jesus Christ God loves us, listens to us and wants to draw us closer to himself. It doesn't mean that we have to learn any new skills or techniques, it doesn't mean that we have to learn a new language, all we have to learn is to talk, to listen and to be still.

Prayer is talking to God as if you were holding a conversation. But it's a conversation in which you know before you start that you will be heard and accepted. The minute you begin, it is as though God is saying his 'Yes' to you. You are affirmed and loved by God right from the start. Of course, as you pray you will discover that whilst prayer is apparently simple it is also full of depth, and you will – if you persevere – discover new ways of praying. Just as there are many ways of knowing a person so there are many ways of coming to know God. And just as with a person there are times for seriousness as well as laughter, so it is with God. Your relationship with God will change and develop as the years unfold and so don't expect your prayers always to be the same or to contain the same sorts of feelings. It is far more lively and demanding than that, and sometimes it's quite a struggle.

A Little Prayer Diary

There will be occasions when you wonder if there's anyone listening; that is a common experience. When that happens, don't give up; instead, ask yourself whether God is wanting you to grow a bit, to try new ways of expressing the relationship. If so, accept the silence as a signpost – not a cul-de-sac – saying 'Try another direction'.

There will also be times when prayer feels a bit like wrestling, wrestling with the darkness, wrestling with fear and with the mystery of God. If that happens, take heart that others have had the same experience and, again, persevere. There are times for patience in prayer but also times to struggle; out of the struggle and the desolation may come another, deeper kind of understanding.

Then there will be times when prayer is neither talking nor listening nor struggling, but when everything seems dead. God feels so absent that it is appalling. What do we do then? It's difficult to find the words to explain, but it's a mixture of perseverance and patience because the absence of God can also feel very like his presence. You may find that at such times you have to use other people's prayers because your own words won't come; you may even find that prayer becomes close to impossible. Remember that you are not alone. The Church throughout the world continues to say its prayers, all those millions and millions of Christians;

let their prayers carry you for a while, and in your own darkness just rest on them and on the knowledge that even in the depths, even when you feel at your lowest ebb, even in the absence of God, in truth God is present.

Christian prayer is also listening, and because prayer and living are all of a piece, you can begin to listen to God by learning to listen to other people. You know how lovely it is when someone gives you their full and undivided attention; try to do the same for others. As you do, you will also discover that your prayer time becomes less a matter of talking and more a matter of listening, but it's a very special kind of listening. It's the sort of listening which takes place when you are with someone you love and you don't need to say anything. Listening to God is like that: quietness, stillness, giving attention to the absolute love of God. Like all prayer, listening prayer takes a lifetime to learn but if you can, in every period of prayer, make a time to listen; in your daily life work hard at listening to others so that you can truly understand them. Listening to God and listening to others are closely linked.

Prayer, then, is talking and listening but it is also being still. Life is now so busy and so frantic that we are losing our human ability to watch and wait, but it's only out of real stillness that great art, music, poetry and science emerge. If we are always in a rush and distracted, we shall miss the stillness at the centre of all things. In your prayer time spend some time each day being still. You don't have to think holy thoughts; all you are doing is placing yourself very quietly in the presence of the God of love and allowing the Holy Spirit to be with you.

This diary is meant to help you make the most of your prayer life. Each day there are suggestions to help you in your prayer conversations as well as prayers which other people have found useful. When you can't find your own words to express what you want to say they may be helpful to you, but don't forget that the more honest and natural your time with God is, the better.

Each of the days also includes a short meditation to help you to think about your relationship with God. At the end of the diary there is some simple advice about using the scripture in prayer, and a selection of short, easy to remember 'arrow' prayers.

Prayer is talking; prayer is listening; prayer is being still, knowing that God is love and longs to draw us close.

Ways of Praying

Just as there are different ways of talking, different dialects and languages, so there are a variety of ways of praying.

An old established form of praying divides prayer into four parts: you can remember it by the word 'ACTS'. A is for adoration, C is for confession, T is for thanksgiving and S is for supplication (which really means 'asking' – another similar word is 'intercession'). Each page in this prayer diary has been divided into these parts, with the addition of a section called 'Dedication'.

Another way of remembering the pattern of prayer is to think of it as a hand. The thumb, because it is the strongest, represents 'God'. The index finger points at others but when it does, three fingers point back at you: so it stands for 'Confession'. The middle finger is the tallest and it represents 'Thanksgiving'. The next finger is 'Others' and the little finger is 'Myself'.

You may discover other patterns of prayer as you progress: but in the next few pages we try to explore the traditional pattern in more detail.

Where you pray is largely up to you: but you will find that somewhere quiet and private is really best (bedroom? bathroom? church?) – somewhere you can think your own thoughts without being disturbed.

A Little Prayer Diary

When you pray will depend to a large extent on how your daily life is organized. It is a good idea to begin each day with a prayer, as a way of committing yourself to God. Before getting up you could say quietly to yourself the Lord's Prayer or a verse from the bible e.g. 'This is the day which the Lord has made, we will rejoice and be glad in it.'

Many people find they pray best at the end of the day when they recall all that has happened and offer it to God. And some people find mid-day a good time: when perhaps they can find a few moments for silence and recollection.

Whether you pray at daybreak, noon or sunset is up to you – but do decide when is best and stick to it.

How long you pray will vary from day to day. Sometimes it will be a few minutes, other days half an hour. Whatever you do, don't rush your prayers; take your time, and remember that you are always in God's presence, held by his love.

Whether you kneel, sit, stand or even lie down depends upon your preference (though lying down leads to sleepiness if you're not careful). What you need to do is to make your body as comfortable as possible so that you can then ignore it. Some people find it very helpful to relax their bodies by deep breathing exercises – but only do that with help from someone more experienced in prayer than you are.

And if your thoughts wander? Don't worry too much – God made us to dream and if you try to force yourself to concentrate you'll discover that your wandering thoughts will find another way of winning. For the moment – be gentle with yourself in your prayer. You have years and years ahead of you to get it right.

ADORATION

It's very easy, well, reasonably easy anyway, to adore something or someone you can see – be it a favourite pet, or a parent, or a pop star. But how do you adore God whom you can't see?

Well: don't be dishonest. Don't try to manufacture feelings of adoration. Don't pretend to be 'in love' with God. Adoration simply means that you try to speak the truth about God to God. At the beginning of each diary page there is a section labelled 'Adoration'. These quotations are as truthful a way of describing God as any human being can find: they bear thinking about, learning and repeating, for they are the distillation of centuries of prayer. As you use the phrases and allow them to sink deeply into your soul, you will discover how accurate, how glorious they are.

Perhaps it might help if you think of God as a landscape – new and unexplored by you. As you explore you discover signposts and markers left by other people who have already been there. These signposts (the

Adoration quotations) don't describe the view or their
feelings: rather they are there to say that you are on
the right track – and that there's more exploring to be
done.

CONFESSION

If adoration sometimes seems difficult, confession is
quite the opposite. You will be well aware of the things
you have said or thought or done which have been
wrong. It's such a relief then to find that you can get
them off your chest and tell God all about them.

Don't wallow in your sins or gloat or make a meal
of them, and certainly don't spend all your time thinking
about them. God knows you better than you know
yourself: you are saying nothing that isn't known already,
but the love in which you are held means that God does
not want you to be burdened by all the things that
trouble you or make you afraid.

You are required to be you (that's why you have been
created uniquely) but God knows that you can also go
against the grain of things, get in a terrible muddle or
deliberately choose to ignore God. So confession has
been given as an opportunity to return to our Creator,
who will meet you with open arms.

So: tell God all and you will be helped to understand
why you are as you are – even though that may take
your whole life to learn.

But 'confession' is not just about individual sins. As human beings we are caught up in a world which sometimes seems crazy, unjust, cruel and arbitrary. When the sins that you commit are simply the sins of all mankind, when the very structures and systems of our world appear to be bent by sin: what then? How shall that be confessed?

The first step is to recognize that that is the case – that you share in the sin of all mankind. The second step is to share that awareness with God (not taking on your shoulders responsibility for everything: that is plainly unrealistic). The third step is to realize that in Jesus Christ God has battled and continues to battle with the sin of the world, as well as your individual sins. And the fourth step is to commit yourself to do something about it, no matter how small; to try to align yourself with God's desire for good and justice everywhere.

THANKSGIVING

If you live thankfully you will live happily. You know how it is if you have a friend who moans all the time. It gets you down. It's boring. But if you live thankfully, that is, aware that everything, absolutely everything has been given by God, you will discover a treasure which will be with you for the rest of your life.

One of the names for the Holy Communion service is 'Eucharist', a Greek word which means 'Thanksgiving'.

That meal, that service, is at the centre of our Christian life – it is filled with thanksgiving.

(Look at your Communion service book and count up how many times thanksgiving is mentioned.) Jesus lived thankfully. Oh yes, he battled with disease and doubt but he lived with thanks to God on his lips and in his life.

In this prayer diary you will find all kinds of suggestions for thanksgiving – they are there as a guide, but do add more as you go along. And keep thankfulness at the centre of your prayers.

SUPPLICATION

Jesus told a story about asking God for things (you will find it in Luke 11:1–13). He encouraged his disciples and followers to ask God for what they wanted (the Lord's Prayer has a number of requests in it) – but he did so in the knowledge that the love of God knows our needs even before we ask. That should be at the root of our asking. God knows our needs. And if we ask things for ourselves we should do so only if we are confident that we can also say 'Thy will be done'.

But what about asking for others? The gospels again provide the pattern for us to follow. Sick people are brought before Jesus by their friends. This is the essence of supplication: simply to carry our requests into the presence of God and leave them there.

Ways of Praying

And if your prayers aren't answered? Well, maybe it isn't right or appropriate that they should be; maybe God knows more about the situation than we do; maybe in love silence is more eloquent than words. When that happens all we can do is hang on in trust and hope. It's often difficult – but we don't really have any other choice, do we?

A Little Prayer Diary

A Little Prayer Diary

Day 1

ADORATION
Glory be to the Father and to the Son
and to the Holy Spirit,
as it was in the beginning,
is now and ever shall be
world without end. Amen.

CONFESSION
O Lord Jesus Christ look upon us with those eyes of
yours, the eyes with which you looked upon Peter in the
hall of judgement, that with Peter we may repent and by
your great love be forgiven and restored; for your
mercy's sake.

Bishop Lancelot Andrewes 1555–1626

THANKSGIVING
Thank God for your home and those who care for you.

INTERCESSION
Pray for any young people you know who may be having
difficulties at home.

DEDICATION

Visit, we beseech thee, O Lord, this place and drive from
it all the snares of the enemy; let your holy angels dwell
here to preserve us in peace and may your blessing be
upon us evermore, through Jesus Christ our Lord.

From Compline

To seek God means first of all
to let your self be found by him.
Rule for a New Brother

Day 2

ADORATION
Holy, holy, holy Lord,
God of power and might,
heaven and earth are full of your glory.
Hosanna in the highest.

CONFESSION
Father, I am very sorry for all that I have said, thought
or done which has not been worthy of a follower of your
Son, our Saviour Jesus Christ.

C. W. Herbert

THANKSGIVING
Thank God for your friends and name them in the
presence of God.

INTERCESSION
Pray for people you know who are lonely.

DEDICATION
May the love of the Lord Jesus draw us to himself; may
the power of the Lord Jesus fill our souls, and may the
blessing of God Almighty, the Father, the Son and the
Holy Spirit be with us and abide with us always.

William Temple, *Parish Prayers*

God is the still point at the centre.
Julian of Norwich b. 1342

Day 3

ADORATION
Praise God from whom all blessings flow,
praise him all creatures here below,
praise him above ye angel host,
praise Father, Son and Holy Ghost.

Bishop Ken 1673–1711

CONFESSION
Give us true repentance: forgive us our sins of
negligence and ignorance and our deliberate sins; and
grant us the grace of your Holy Spirit to amend our lives
according to your holy word.

ASB 1980

THANKSGIVING
Thank God for your leisure activities; sport, games,
reading, watching television.

INTERCESSION
Pray for the very old, especially for those whose
interests have, through age, become limited.

DEDICATION
Here I am Lord – body, heart and soul.
Grant that with your love,
I may be big enough to reach the world
and small enough to be at one with you.

Mother Teresa

We can do no great things – only small things with
great love...nothing is small for God because he is
almighty and therefore each one of our actions done
with and through Jesus Christ is a great success.
Mother Teresa

Day 4

ADORATION
Lord, you are holy indeed,
the source of all holiness.

CONFESSION
Holy God – have mercy upon those faults I share with all
    mankind
holy and strong – have mercy upon the strong and the
    powerful
holy and immortal – have mercy upon the rich and the
    wealthy
have mercy upon us – have mercy upon our unjust and
    unhappy world, for Jesus' sake.

THANKSGIVING
Thank God for your own health and strength.

INTERCESSION
Pray for those who care for the sick: for your own
doctor, for any hospitals in your area.

Day 4

DEDICATION
Lord thou knowest how busy I must be this day.
If I forget thee do not thou forget me.

Lord Astley, before the battle of Edgehill 1642

The best prayer is to rest in the goodness of God
knowing that that goodness can reach right down to
our lowest depths of need.
Julian of Norwich b. 1342

Day 5

ADORATION
My soul waits in silence for God,
for from him comes my salvation.

Psalm 62:1

CONFESSION
Almighty and everlasting God, who hatest nothing
that thou hast made, and dost forgive the sins of all
them that are penitent: create and make in us new and
contrite hearts, that we worthily lamenting our sins and
acknowledging our wretchedness, may obtain of thee,
the God of all mercy, perfect remission and forgiveness;
through Jesus Christ our Lord.

Book of Common Prayer

THANKSGIVING
Thank God for the freedom you enjoy: to speak, to think,
to express yourself.

INTERCESSION
Pray for all who are imprisoned unjustly by reason of
their political and religious beliefs. Pray for all those
who work for their well-being.

DEDICATION
O God, stay with me; let no word cross my lips that is
not your word, no thoughts enter my mind that are not
your thoughts, no deed ever be done or entertained by
me that is not your deed.

                    Malcolm Muggeridge, *Jesus Rediscovered*

I believe in the sun even when it is not shining
I believe in love, even when I cannot feel it
I believe in God even when he is silent.
Written on a wall by a Jewish prisoner in Cologne

Day 6

ADORATION
O shout with joy to God all the earth:
sing to the honour of his name
and give him glory as his praise.

Psalm 66:1–2

CONFESSION
Merciful Lord, grant to your faithful people
pardon and peace
that we may be cleansed from all our sins
and serve you with a quiet mind
through Jesus Christ our Lord.

ASB 1980

THANKSGIVING
Thank God for the music you enjoy: for all who make
music and all in the recording industry.

INTERCESSION
Pray for any musicians you know and especially for
anyone whose music has given you pleasure.

DEDICATION
My God, I am not my own but yours.
Take me for your own
and help me in all things to do your holy will.
My God I give myself to you
in joy and in sorrow
in sickness and in health
in success and in failure
in life and in death
in time and for eternity.
Make me and keep me your own
through Jesus Christ our Lord.

What does the Lord require of you but to do justly,
to love mercy and to walk humbly with your God?
Micah 6:8

Day 7

ADORATION

We praise thee, O God;
We acknowledge thee to be the Lord.
All the earth doth worship thee,
the Father everlasting.

Te Deum

CONFESSION

Almighty...
Forgive
my doubt
my anger
my pride.
By thy mercy
abase me,
in thy strictness
raise me up.

Dag Hammarskjöld 1905–1961, *Markings*

THANKSGIVING

Thank God for the art you enjoy: for any painting or
sculpture you particularly like.

Day 7

INTERCESSION
Pray for any artists you know: for students and teachers
at colleges of art.

DEDICATION
Into thy hands, O Lord, I commend my spirit, now and
for evermore.

Following Jesus means following the path he took and
seeing things as he saw them.
Rule for a New Brother

Day 8

ADORATION

Lord God of our ancestor Jacob, may you be praised for ever and ever! You are great and powerful, glorious, splendid and majestic. Everything in heaven and earth is yours and you are king, supreme ruler over all.

1 Chronicles 29:10–11

CONFESSION

Lord, for thy tender mercies' sake, lay not our sins to our charge but forgive that which is past and give us grace to amend our sinful lives; to decline from sin and incline to virtue, that we may walk with a perfect heart before thee, now and evermore.

Ridley's Prayers: 1566

THANKSGIVING

Thank God for comedians – and for anyone who makes you laugh and enjoy life.

INTERCESSION

Pray for anyone you know who finds life weary and burdensome, hard and heavy.

DEDICATION

Teach us, good Lord, to serve thee as thou deservest: to give and not to count the cost; to fight and not to heed the wounds; to toil and not to seek for rest; to labour and not to ask for any reward save that of knowing that we do thy will, through the same Jesus Christ our Lord.

St Ignatius 1491–1556

You are unique, irreplaceable.
Did you know that? Why aren't you surprised?
Why aren't you glad, astonished about yourself
and about everyone else you know?
Phil Bosmans, *Give Happiness a Chance*

Day 9

ADORATION

Holy, holy, holy, is the Lord God almighty
who was, who is, and who is to come.

Revelation 4:8

CONFESSION

Lord Jesus Christ, Son of God
have mercy on me, a sinner.
forgive those sins which are mine alone
forgive those sins I have in common with everyone
forgive those sins which prevent others from knowing
     you.
Lord Jesus Christ, Son of God,
have mercy on us all.

THANKSGIVING

Thank God for your church – for the people you meet
there and for those who have helped you in your
Christian life.

INTERCESSION

Pray for the work of your local church and for its
leaders.

DEDICATION
I hand over to your care, Lord
my soul and body
my mind and thoughts
my prayers and my hopes
my health and my work
my life and my death
my parents and my family
my friends and my neighbours
my country and all men
today and for ever.

Bishop Lancelot Andrewes 1555–1626

Christ is the morning star
who when the darkness of this world is past
brings to his saints
the promise of the light of life
and opens everlasting day.
The Venerable Bede 672–735

Day 10

ADORATION
Our Lord and God! You are worthy to receive glory and honour and power. For you created all things, and by your will they were given existence and life.

Revelation 4:11

CONFESSION
Father, forgive me.

THANKSGIVING
Thank God for the Bible – for all who have worked and suffered that you might be able to read it.

INTERCESSION
Pray for all who print and produce Bibles and distribute them throughout the world. Pray for all who, because of the regime under which they live, have no access to a Bible.

DEDICATION
Lord, I believe,
help thou mine unbelief.

If we know how to listen to God,
if we know how to look around us,
our whole life would become prayer.
Michel Quoist, *Prayers of Life*

Day 11

ADORATION

To him who by means of his power working in us is able
to do so much more than we can ever ask for, or even
think of: to God be the glory in the Church and in Christ
Jesus for all time, for ever and ever! Amen.

Ephesians 3:20–21

CONFESSION

Jesus, Lord Christ
you lived for us
you died for us;
make me like you.
Save me, free me from sin:
give me your strength.

THANKSGIVING

Thank God for the gift of hearing.

INTERCESSION

Pray for those you know who are deaf: for all research
into deafness; for all doctors, teachers, nurses, social
workers and priests ministering to the deaf.

DEDICATION

Lord, make me a channel of your peace,
that where there is hatred I may bring love;
that where there is wrong I may bring the spirit of
    forgiveness;
that where there is discord I may bring harmony;
that where there is error I may bring truth;
that where there is despair I may bring hope;
that where there are shadows I may bring light;
that where there is sadness I may bring joy.

                    attributed to St Francis of Assisi 1181–1226

If we really want to pray, we must first learn to
listen, for in the silence of the heart God speaks.
Mother Teresa

Day 12

ADORATION
How great are God's riches! How deep are his wisdom and knowledge!

Romans 11:33

CONFESSION
Lord, have mercy upon us.
Christ, have mercy upon us.
Lord, have mercy upon us.

THANKSGIVING
Thank God for the time you have already spent on this earth and recall moments of special happiness.

INTERCESSION
Pray for those who have a limited and known time to live; for their friends and families.

DEDICATION
May God the Father bless us; may Christ take care of us,
the Holy Spirit enlighten us all the days of our life.
The Lord be our defender and keeper now and for ever.

Prayers of St Hedelward 753–827

God does not hurry over things; time is his, not mine.
And I, little creature, have been called
to be transformed into God by sharing his life.
And what transforms me is the charity
which he pours into my heart.
Love transforms me slowly into God.
Carlo Carretto, *Letters from the Desert*

Day 13

ADORATION
I will proclaim your greatness, my God and king.
I will thank you for ever and ever.

Psalm 145:1

CONFESSION
Remove my sin, and I will be clean;
wash me and I will be whiter than snow
...close your eyes to my sins
and wipe out all my evil.

Psalm 51:7.9

THANKSGIVING
Thank God for books you have enjoyed or which have
been helpful to you.

INTERCESSION
Pray for those people who, because of the poverty of
their country, have no books and maybe cannot read.

DEDICATION
Lord, increase my faith
bless my efforts and work
now and for evermore.

Mother Teresa

Were the whole realm of nature mine
that were an offering far too small.
Love so amazing, so divine
demands my soul, my life, my all.
Isaac Watts 1674–1748

Day 14

ADORATION
Praise the Lord!
Praise the Lord, my soul.
I will praise him as long as I live...

Psalm 146:1

CONFESSION
O Lord, look upon me with love and mercy
forgive me, cleanse me, restore me
that I may praise your name
for ever and ever.

THANKSGIVING
Thank God for those who look after you like a mother.

INTERCESSION
Pray for anyone you know who feels unloved and
unwanted.

Day 14

DEDICATION
Grant, O Lord God, that we may
cleave to thee without parting;
worship thee without wearying;
serve thee without failing.
Faithfully seek thee.
Happily find thee.
For ever possess thee
the only one God
bless'd world without end.

St Anselm 1033–1109

As truly as God is our father,
so just as truly is he our mother.
Julian of Norwich b. 1342

Day 15

ADORATION
Sing a new song to the Lord,
Sing his praise all the world.

Isaiah 42:10

CONFESSION
Father, I turn to you and ask for forgiveness
knowing that your love is infinite, your mercy eternal...
I remember the poor, the hungry, the homeless, the
tortured, and all the sadness of our world. Forgive the
part we all play in this – and in your love strengthen us
that we may work for justice, through Jesus Christ
our Lord.

THANKSGIVING
Thank God for the area in which you live: those parts of
it which are special to you and of which you feel proud.

INTERCESSION
Pray for all refugees; for those who by reason of famine
or war or disaster have had to uproot.

DEDICATION
Night is drawing nigh;
for all that has been, thanks,
to all that shall be, yes.

Dag Hammarskjöld 1905–1961, *Markings*

The God of love my shepherd is
and he that doth me feed.
While he is mine and I am his
what can I want or need?
Psalm 23, George Herbert

Day 16

ADORATION
My heart praises the Lord; my soul is glad because of God my Saviour...

Luke 1:46–47

CONFESSION
Save me, O Lord, from myself.

THANKSGIVING
Thank God for your emotions, for your feelings; whether of love or of anger, whether of peace or frustration.

INTERCESSION
Pray for those people who find their emotions very difficult and who feel deeply confused.

DEDICATION
O heavenly Father, protect and bless all things that have breath, guard them from evil and let them sleep in peace.

Albert Schweitzer

Don't try to reach God with your understanding,
that is impossible.
Reach him in love, that is possible.
Carlo Carretto, *Letters from the Desert*

Day 17

ADORATION

Glory to God in the highest heaven, peace on earth to those with whom he is pleased.

Luke 2:14

CONFESSION

Almighty God, our heavenly Father,
we have sinned against you and against our
fellow men in thought and word and deed,
through negligence, through weakness,
through our own deliberate fault.
We are truly sorry
and repent of all our sins.
For the sake of your Son Jesus Christ who died for us,
forgive us all that is past;
and grant that we may serve you in newness of life,
to the glory of your name. Amen.

ASB 1980

THANKSGIVING

Thank God for those who earn money that you might be fed and clothed and housed.

INTERCESSION
Pray for those with whom you work, pray for the
unemployed, and for all involved in industrial relations.

DEDICATION
Christ beneath me, Christ above me,
Christ in quiet, Christ in danger,
Christ in hearts of all that love me
Christ in mouth of friend or stranger.

St Patrick 390–461

The Father has put us into the world, not to walk
through it with lowered eyes,
but to search for him through things, events, people.
Everything must reveal God to us.
Michel Quoist, *Prayers of Life*

Day 18

ADORATION
My Lord and my God.

John 20:28

CONFESSION
Be merciful to me, O God
because of your constant love.
Because of your great mercy
wipe away my sins!
Wash away all my evil
and make me clean from my sins.

Psalm 51:1–2

THANKSGIVING
Thank God for the talents and gifts he has given you.

INTERCESSION
Pray for all those who feel that their lives are useless
and have no meaning or value.

DEDICATION
The Lord is my light and my salvation;
I will fear no one.
The Lord protects me from all danger;
I will never be afraid.

Psalm 27:1

Don't be afraid or discouraged, for I, the Lord your God,
am with you wherever you go.
Joshua 1:9

Day 19

ADORATION
Praise, glory, wisdom, thanksgiving, honour, power, and might belong to our God for ever and ever.

Revelation 7:12

CONFESSION
Most merciful God, we have sinned in thought and word
    and deed:
we are truly sorry and we ask you to forgive us.
Help us by your spirit to live a new life in Christ,
loving you with all our heart,
and our neighbour as ourselves,
for Jesus Christ's sake.

Cyril Taylor & David Silk

THANKSGIVING
Thank God for his Son, Jesus Christ – for all you have learnt about him, for his presence with you.

INTERCESSION
Pray for those who have not yet found faith and for those who have lost their faith.

DEDICATION
Like an eagle gliding upon the rising air
Uphold me with your presence Lord.

C. W. Herbert, *The Edge of Wonder*

A Christian doesn't think God will love us
because we're good, but that God will make us good
because he loves us.
C. S. Lewis 1898–1963, *Broadcast Talks*

Day 20

ADORATION

God is wise and powerful!
praise him for ever and ever.
He controls the times and the seasons;
he makes and unmakes kings,
it is he who gives wisdom and understanding.

Daniel 2:20–21

CONFESSION

Jesus, Lamb of God: have mercy on us
Jesus, bearer of our sins: have mercy on us
Jesus, redeemer of the world: give us your peace.

ASB 1980

THANKSGIVING

Thank God for the saints of our country: for the saint
after whom your church is named, for your patron saint.

INTERCESSION

Pray for anyone you know who may be working with the
Church abroad. Pray for the bishop of your diocese or
your Church's leaders.

DEDICATION
Christ be with me, Christ within me
Christ behind me, Christ before me
Christ beside me, Christ to win me
Christ to comfort and restore me...

St Patrick 390–461

*If you abide in love you will abide in God and not
wander anymore in darkness.*
Rule for a New Brother

Day 21

ADORATION

God reveals things that are deep and secret;
he knows what is hidden in darkness,
and he himself is surrounded by light.

Daniel 2:22

CONFESSION

Almighty God,
to whom all hearts are open,
all desires known,
and from whom no secrets are hidden;
cleanse the thoughts of our hearts
by the inspiration of your Holy Spirit
that we may perfectly love you
and worthily magnify your holy name,
through Christ our Lord.

ASB 1980

THANKSGIVING

Thank God for the science you know and for the many
benefits science and technology have brought to our
world.

INTERCESSION
Pray for any scientists you know and for all who have to
make difficult decisions in their work.

DEDICATION
O most merciful redeemer, friend and brother,
may I know thee more clearly
love thee more dearly
and follow thee more nearly, day by day.
                    St Richard of Chichester 1197–1253

Christian prayer is not an attempt to use God for
our purposes but a petition that he will use us for his.
              Archbishop William Temple 1881–1944

Day 22

ADORATION
Praise the Lord, my Soul!
O Lord, my God, how great you are!
You are clothed with majesty and glory;
you cover yourself with light.

Psalm 104:1

CONFESSION
Lord, I repent of my sins.

THANKSGIVING
Thank God for the gifts of the earth, for its resources of
minerals and metals, oil and food...

INTERCESSION
Pray for a fair and just distribution of those resources.
O Lord,
so many sick
so many starving
so many deprived
so many sad
so many bitter
so many fearful
when I look at them

my heart fails
when I look at you
I hope again.
Help me to help you to
reduce the world's
pain.
O God of infinite
compassion.
O ceaseless energy of love.

George Appleton, *Prayers from a Troubled Heart*

DEDICATION
May the Lord bless us,
may he keep us from all evil
and lead us to life everlasting.

We are the wire, God is the current.
Our only power is to let the current pass through us;
of course, we have the power to interrupt it and say 'No'.
But nothing more.
Carlo Carretto, *Letters from the Desert*

Day 23

ADORATION
Sing to the Lord, all the world!
Worship the Lord with joy;
come before him with happy songs.

Psalm 100:1

CONFESSION
We confess to God almighty, the Father, the Son and the Holy Ghost, that we have sinned in thought, word and deed, through our own grievous fault. Wherefore we pray God to have mercy upon us.

Book of Common Prayer (1928)

THANKSGIVING
Thank God for the great seasons of the year: for spring, summer, autumn and winter.

INTERCESSION
Pray for farmers and market gardeners and all involved in the food industry.

DEDICATION
O Lord support us all the day long of this troublous life until the shadows lengthen and the evening comes, the busy world is hushed, the fever of life is over and our work is done. Then, Lord, in thy mercy grant us a safe lodging, a holy rest and peace at the last through Jesus Christ...

Book of Common Prayer (1928)

It is Christmas every time you smile at someone and offer them your hand... it is Christmas every time you let God love others through you.
Mother Teresa

Day 24

ADORATION
God is my saviour; I will trust him and not be afraid.
The Lord gives me power and strength; he is my saviour.

Isaiah 12:2

CONFESSION
If you forgive others the wrongs they have done to you,
your Father in heaven will also forgive you. But if you do
not forgive others, then your Father will not forgive the
wrongs you have done.

Matthew 6:14–15

Father, teach me forgiveness.

THANKSGIVING
Thank God for the things that are good about your
country.

INTERCESSION
Pray for all who make and enforce law, that they may be
wise, just and merciful.

DEDICATION
God made me.
God loves me and keeps me
gives comfort and grace
for every need
at every moment
on and around me
within me. Thanks be to God.

George Appleton, *Prayers from a Troubled Heart*

It seems that enquiry and commitment must go
forward together hand—in—hand; continuously side—
by—side. It is a very difficult task to keep them
more or less level but I can't see any other way to
make honest progress.
Philip Toynbee, *Part of a Journey*

Day 25

ADORATION
God, with all my heart I trust you,
with all my mind I love you.
Strengthen me with your peace, for Jesus' sake.

C. W. Herbert, *The Edge of Wonder*

CONFESSION
Lord, forgive what we have been, help us to amend what
we are and direct what we shall be...and, Lord, help me
to understand what 'we' implies...

Joint Liturgical Group (adapted)

THANKSGIVING
Thank God for all who work with and for young people;
for teachers, youth leaders, counsellors.

INTERCESSION
Pray for young people's groups in your area and in
particular for the leaders.

DEDICATION
May the love of the Lord Jesus draw us to himself,
may the power of the Lord Jesus strengthen us in his
service,
may the joy of the Lord Jesus fill our hearts.

Joint Liturgical Group, Daily Office

When you go to sleep
bury all that has happened in the mercy of God.
It will be safe there.
Stand back from what has happened,
and be grateful for it all.
Rule for a New Brother

Day 26

ADORATION

Be thou, my vision, O Lord of my heart.
Be all else but naught to me, save that thou art,
be thou my best thought in the day and the night
both waking and sleeping, thy presence my light.

Irish 8th century

CONFESSION

From the depths of my despair,
I call to you, Lord.
Hear my cry, O Lord;
listen to my call for help.

Psalm 130:1

THANKSGIVING

Thank God for the gift of the Holy Spirit: whose
presence renews you at all times and in all places.

INTERCESSION

Pray for those who are mentally ill and for those who
care for them: for all research into mental illness.

DEDICATION
O Lord, guard us waking and keep us sleeping; that awake we may watch with Christ and asleep we may rest in peace.

from Compline

Loneliness is being unaware of One
that is with us everywhere.
E. A. Gloeggler

Day 27

ADORATION
God is love: let heaven adore him;
God is love: let earth rejoice;
let creation sing before him,
and exalt him with one voice.

Timothy Rees 1874–1939

CONFESSION
Lamb of God, you take away the sins of the world:
    have mercy on us.
Lamb of God, you take away the sins of the world:
    have mercy on us.
Lamb of God, you take away the sins of the world:
    grant us peace.

THANKSGIVING
Thank God for anyone who has helped you recently
when you had a problem.

INTERCESSION
Pray for all social workers and community leaders and
those who work to create neighbourliness in your area.

DEDICATION
Lead me from death to life, from falsehood to truth.
Lead me from despair to hope, from fear to trust.
Lead me from hate to love, from war to peace.
Let peace fill our heart, our world, our universe.

When I needed a neighbour were you there, were you there?
When I needed a neighbour were you there?
Sydney Carter

Day 28

ADORATION

Let all the world in every corner sing:
my God and King!
The heavens are not too high,
his praise may thither fly;
the earth is not too low,
his praises there may grow.
Let all the world in every corner sing:
my God and King!

George Herbert 1593–1633

CONFESSION

May the almighty and merciful Lord grant unto us
pardon and remission of all our sins, time for amendment
of life, and the grace and comfort of the Holy Spirit.

from Compline

THANKSGIVING

Thank God for the special interests you have developed
and are developing either at work or in your leisure time.

INTERCESSION
Pray for all involved in careers advice and especially for those who have helped you in your decision making.

DEDICATION
Eternal God and Father, by whose power we are created and by whose love we are redeemed: guide and strengthen us by thy Spirit that we may give ourselves to thy service and live this day in love to one another and to thee through Jesus Christ our Lord.

Joint Liturgical Group

Don't walk in front of me, I may not follow.
Don't walk behind me, I may not lead.
Just walk beside me and be my friend.

Day 29

ADORATION
Fill thou my life, O Lord my God,
in every part with praise,
that my whole being may proclaim
thy being and thy ways.

H. Bonar 1808–89

CONFESSION
O God,
we ask you to forgive us for
the things we have not thought about,
the jobs we have not done,
the words we have not spoken.
We ask you to help us
to think
and do
and say
the right things at the right times.

Pray With

THANKSGIVING
Thank God for the gift of prayer.

INTERCESSION
Pray that God will help you to develop and enrich your
relationship with him.

DEDICATION
The grace of our Lord Jesus Christ and the love of God
and the fellowship of the Holy Spirit be with us all
evermore. Amen.

The prayer of a Christian is prayer with all the saints.
Archbishop Michael Ramsey

Day 30

ADORATION

How great are God's riches! How deep are his wisdom
and knowledge!... For all things were created by him,
and all things exist through him and for him. To God be
the glory for ever! Amen.

Romans 11:33, 36

CONFESSION

O most holy God,
you know me better than I know myself,
forgive what needs forgiveness
strengthen what is weak
and give me wisdom for Jesus' sake.

THANKSGIVING

Thank God that he is God.

INTERCESSION

Pray for all who work in difficult environments: for
sailors, aircrew, soldiers, police, miners, nurses...

DEDICATION
I find prayer so powerful
that I need but one:
heavenly Father
grant me the wisdom
to see the good
in everyone
and everything.
You know my needs:
I do not need to ask,
I appreciate your gifts. Amen.

James Haylock Eyre, in *Beyond all Pain*

I said to the man who stood at the Gate of the Year,
'Give me a light that I may tread safely into the
unknown.' And he replied: 'Go out into the darkness
and put your hand into the hand of God. That shall be
to you better than light and safer than a known way.'
Minnie Haskins 1875–1957

Day 31

ADORATION
Yours Lord is the greatness, the power, the glory, the splendour and the majesty. For everything in heaven and on earth is yours: all things come from you and of your own do we give you.

ASB 1980

CONFESSION
O Saviour of the World, who by thy cross and precious blood hast redeemed us: save us and help us we humbly beseech thee, O Lord.

Book of Common Prayer

THANKSGIVING
Thank God for all you have learnt so far on your own pilgrimage to him.

INTERCESSION
Pray for your fellow-pilgrims and especially for those who are sharing your journey at the moment.

DEDICATION
God be in my head and in my understanding;
God be in my eyes and in my looking;
God be in my mouth and in my speaking;
God be at my end and at my departing.

Richard Pynson

Life is a pilgrimage. We are on the march, and
sooner or later we shall reach our destination. That
destination we call heaven. There we shall see God
as he is, and that experience will be the cause of a
happiness which will be complete and have no end.
We are made for that.
Cardinal Basil Hume, *To be a Pilgrim*

Using the Scriptures in prayer

When you read the bible don't put your intelligence on one side. Study the bible with the help of commentaries and notes (ask your minister or priest for advice on which ones to choose), and work hard at understanding it. You will not be disappointed. It is a rich and wonderful treasure house.

But don't only approach the scriptures through your mind. You can use scriptures in your prayer as well. How? There are several ways.

Let's begin with the simplest first. When you read a bible passage read it carefully and quietly and wait to see which particular verse seems to catch your eye. (You may need to read the passage several times.) When that happens just let the verse sink into your thinking; reflect on it, ask questions about it, ponder it. Then weave that verse into a prayer by saying something like; 'Father, thank you for all that I have learnt from (   ). Help me to see how I ought to live my life in the light of its truth.'

The second way of approaching scripture in prayer is by using a method which St Ignatius taught. Picture the scene where the incident in the bible took place.

Imagine you are there – the sounds, the heat, the other people. Ask God to help you to imagine it in such a way that you really feel a part of it. Then think carefully about the passage; try to understand its meaning and ask yourself, 'What does this passage imply about how I ought to live – today, tomorrow, next week...?' Finally commit everything you have learnt from the text to God in a prayer that sums it all up.

A third way of praying with the scriptures is this. Read the passage several times and select one aspect of Jesus' life – e.g. his power, his kindness – which you can then think about for a while. Once you have done that remember that Jesus gives himself to you, and shares with you his gifts – including the attributes you have been thinking about. Then ask God to show you how you may best work with Christ so that those gifts can be shared generously and sensitively with others.

These are three very simple ways of praying with the scriptures. Perhaps before embarking upon them, you could ask someone who is more experienced in prayer to help you in your choice.

Remember, when you pray using the scriptures you aren't trying to impress yourself (or God) with clever techniques, nor are you abandoning your intelligence. What you are trying to do is simply to make yourself available to God and to listen to his word so that you may live in his way.

Arrow Prayers

'Arrow' prayers are very simple prayers which you can fire off, as it were, in a split second. You might like to learn some of them:

- This is the day which the Lord has made, we will rejoice and be glad in it.

- Send out thy light and thy truth, let them lead me.

- Be still and know what I am God.

- The Lord is my shepherd; there is nothing I shall want.

- Where two or three are gathered together in my name, there am I in the midst of them.

- Lo, I am with you always to the end of time.

- Into thy hands I commend my spirit.

- Lord, you are with us always.

A Little Prayer Diary

- Nothing in life or death can separate me from your love.

- O Thou.

- Lord Jesus have mercy on me, sinner that I am.

- Word of God, speak within me.

- Here am I, send me.

- Lord, you surround me with your love.

- The Lord is here: His Spirit is with us.

- Lord of the stillness, give me your peace.

- The Lord is my strength and my song.

- I know that my redeemer liveth.

Useful Prayers

THE TEN COMMANDMENTS

You shall have no other gods before me.

You shall not make for yourself a graven image.

You shall not take the name of the Lord your God in vain.

Remember the Sabbath day, to keep it holy.

Honour your father and your mother.

You shall not kill.

You shall not commit adultery.

You shall not steal.

You shall not bear false witness against your neighbour.

You shall not covet.

THE LAW OF LOVE

A teacher of the Law was there who heard the discussion. He saw that Jesus had given the Sadducees a good answer, so he came to him with a question: 'Which commandment is the most important of all?'

Jesus replied, 'The most important one is this, "Listen, Israel! The Lord our God is the only Lord. Love the Lord your God with all your heart, with all your soul, with all your mind, and with all your strength." The second most important commandment is this: "Love your neighbour as you love yourself." There is no commandment more important than these two.'

Mark 12:28–31

THE GOLDEN RULE

Do unto others as you would have them do unto you.